Westminster Abbey: The History of England's Most Famous Church

By Dr. Jesse Harasta and Charles River Editors

About Charles River Editors

Charles River Editors provides superior editing and original writing services across the digital publishing industry, with the expertise to create digital content for publishers across a vast range of subject matter. In addition to providing original digital content for third party publishers, we also republish civilization's greatest literary works, bringing them to new generations of readers via ebooks.

Sign up here to receive updates about free books as we publish them, and visit Our Kindle Author Page to browse today's free promotions and our most recently published Kindle titles.

Introduction

Westminster Abbey

"It is eerie being all but alone in Westminster Abbey. Without the tourists, there are only the dead, many of them kings and queens. They speak powerfully and put my thoughts into vivid perspective." – A.N. Wilson

It almost goes without saying that Westminster Abbey is one of the foremost sites in Europe when it comes to being steeped in history. Dating back to the reign of William the Conqueror and the Norman conquest, Westminster Abbey has traditionally been the site of royal coronations, royal weddings, and royal burials, and anyone who enters can instantly feel that they are walking in the footsteps of some of the most influential figures in history, from Henry III to Queen Elizabeth I.

Of course, Westminster Abbey is also far more than a place for royalty. As the English became to more intimately associate the site with their history and culture, luminaries from all walks of life have also been interred there, from Charles Darwin and Isaac Newton to Rudyard Kipling and Charles Dickens. Along with effigies, plaques, and various other monuments, walking through Westminster Abbey offers its own sort of crash course on England over the centuries.

While Westminster Abbey has been an important site for nearly 1,000 years, it is perhaps unsurprising that it has had a volatile history, a byproduct of England's own tumultuous past. As a religious site first and foremost, the Abbey was at the forefront of the religious unrest that occasionally swept the British Isles, whether it was Henry VIII's formation of the Church of England or his devoutly Catholic daughter earning the sobriquet Bloody Mary. As a result of it all, the Abbey has served different religious purposes over the course of time as well.

Westminster Abbey: The History of England's Most Famous Church looks at the history of the church from the Middle Ages to today and offers a tour of the different things that visitors will find there. Along with pictures of important people, places, and events, you will learn about Westminster Abbey like never before, in no time at all.

Westminster Abbey: The History of England's Most Famous Church

About Charles River Editors

Introduction

   Traditional Features of a Church

   Chapter 1: The Dark Ages and Origins of the Church

   Chapter 2: Edward the Confessor and Westminster Abbey

   Chapter 3: Henry III and the Current Construction

   Chapter 4: Tudor Dissolution and an Abbey in Name Only

   Chapter 5: Foundations of the Modern Church

   Chapter 6: The Abbey in the 20th and 21st Centuries

   Chapter 7: Tour of the Church

   Bibliography

Traditional Features of a Church

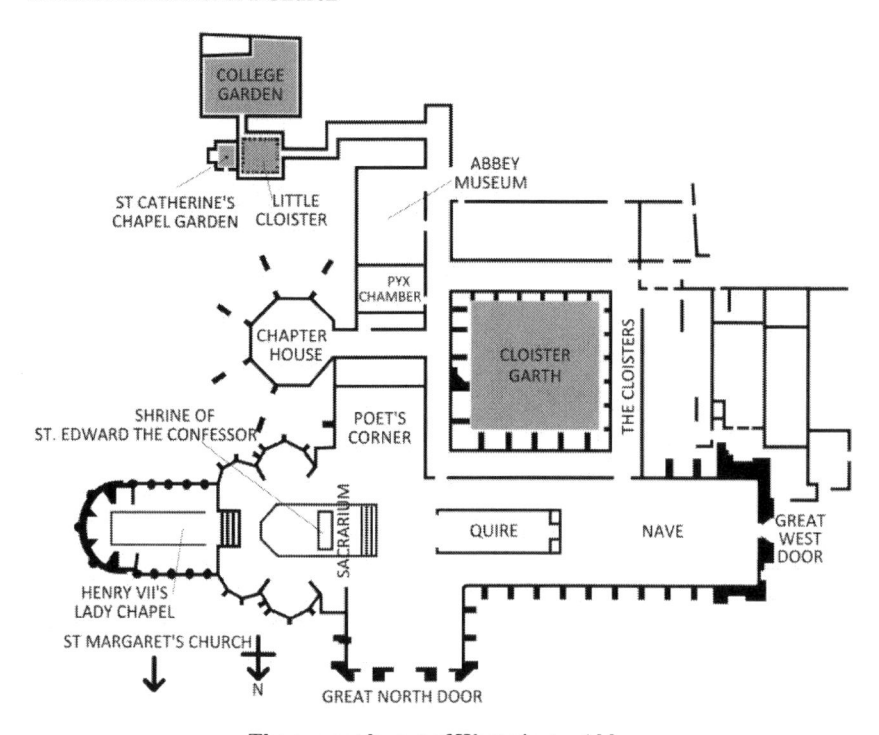

The current layout of Westminster Abbey

"I mean, you can't walk down the aisle in Westminster Abbey in a strapless dress, it just won't happen - it has to suit the grandeur of that aisle, it's enormous." – Bruce Oldfield

Nave: The long main body of the Church, in most Christian churches it is where the majority of the congregation sits in pews.

Herry Lawford's picture of the Nave

Aisle: A long passageway that runs alongside the nave, separated from this main area by a colonnade of columns. The ceilings of the aisle are often lower than that of the nave which has a clerestory above it.

Chancel: An area around and behind the principal altar which, in Westminster and many churches is topped by an apse. The chancel is considered to be sacred space and is often physically separated from the worshipper and accessible only by priests.

Clerestory: A row of windows, usually clear, set high up in the walls of the church, above the primary stained glass and the level of the aisle. The clerestory is designed to bring light into the sanctuary.

Font: A bowl on a pedestal, reminiscent of a large stone birdbath, where baptisms occur in traditions like Anglican Church where baptism is done on infants or small children. It often has its own side chapel.

Lectern: A stand on floor the level where a large copy of the Bible is held for use in readings during Mass. In Anglican churches like Westminster, it is often made of brass and shaped like a soaring eagle - the symbol of John the Evangelist.

Apse: An area behind the main altar of the church, usually a semi-circular domed area; it is separated from the Nave by the Transept.

Transept: If the main body of a traditional Cross-shaped Church like Westminster is the nave, the shorter piece that crosses it near the altar is the Transept. The transept often holds numerous side-chapels.

Choir/Quire: The area of a church where the choir and the clergy sit, separated from the main body of worshipers. In large traditional churches like Westminster, it is often located within the nave close to the transept and blocks the view of the altar of visitors entering the church.

A 19th century illustration of the choir

Pulpit: A raised stand or box, separated from the floor by a small flight of steps. This is where the presiding clergy member delivers the sermon. Before electronic amplification, they were designed to amplify the speaker's voice.

Chapter 1: The Dark Ages and Origins of the Church

Like all ancient churches, the exact foundation and origins of Westminster Abbey is lost to the mists of time. Traditional legend holds that it was founded by Sebert, the King of the East Saxons, in 616 AD during the throes of his people's conversion to Christianity. Sebert (sometimes spelled "Saberht") was said to have also founded the original St. Paul's downriver in London. Much older churches than this are not to be found in England because the Saxon invaders were worshippers of the old Norse/Germanic gods and were thus considered the scourges of the Christians. Sebert was the first Christian king of his people, so any churches from the Roman period (and they would have been relatively few considering the marginal position and early fall of Roman Britain) did not survive into the Saxon period.[1]

Sebert chose a place several miles upriver from the existing site of the City of London on an island called the Isle of Thorney. The name "westminster" is a simple one: "west" for the direction from London, and "minster" being an Old English term for a monastery. According to legend, St. Peter miraculously appeared to consecrate the newly completed church, which has since been dedicated to him.[2]

That said, there is no written or archaeological evidence to corroborate the foundation of Westminster Abbey during Sebert's reign. The primary historian of the Saxon period, the Venerable Bede (672-735), wrote during the early 700s but never mentioned the church, and while that does not necessarily preclude its existence, a church with a royal foundation would have been an important site at the time.

The first hard, datable evidence associated with the building is a charter for a monastery named Westminster (and differentiated specifically from St. Paul's) granted by King Offa of Mercia (757-796) in 785. Other early dates for the church come from a 10th century charter granted by King Edgar the Peaceful of Wessex (943-975), in which the territories controlled by the monastery are more clearly delineated. Additionally, there is a traditional date of 960; according to the historian William of Malmesbury (1095-1143), St. Dunstan (909-988) brought 12 Benedictine monks to the monastery from the ancient monastic seat of Glastonbury and expanded the existing monastery. However, while Westminster definitely emerged as a major seat of the Order of St. Benedict, the story of St. Dunstan has as little corroboration as the original foundation by King Sebert three centuries earlier.

---

1 "Westminster Abbey" at *The Encyclopedia Britannica*. Accessed online at:
http://www.britannica.com/EBchecked/topic/641068/Westminster-Abbey
2 "Westminster Abbey" at *The New Catholic Encyclopedia*. Accessed online at:
http://www.newadvent.org/cathen/15598a.htm

Unfortunately, scholars cannot consult archaeological evidence for help because the exact site of the original monastic structure has been lost, and wherever it was, it has been undoubtedly buried by construction over several centuries.

Chapter 2: Edward the Confessor and Westminster Abbey

Kjetil Bjørnsrud's picture of Edward's Throne

Medieval depiction of Edward the Confessor

There is no figure more important to the history of Westminster Abbey, no individual who shaped its destiny and identity, more than Saint/King Edward "the Confessor" of the House of Wessex, who ruled as king of a united England from 1033-1065. The last universally recognized king of his line[3] before the Norman Conquest, Edward set the stage for the Normans and has served as a symbol of unity with the Saxon past ever since. Ironically, for a king so closely associated with Westminster, it might come as a surprise that Edward did not have his coronation at Westminster but instead at Winchester Cathedral, a major ecclesiastical site during that era. In fact, Edward was the last king in English history up until the present day who did not have his coronation in Westminster.

Edward had a tumultuous reign, and as a child he was forced into exile by Norse conquests. Edward hid in Normandy, where his family had holdings, and during this period abroad, the young king took an oath to make a pilgrimage to Rome if he was reinstated to his throne. Upon his success, he appealed to the Pope to absolve him of this vow, but while the Pope did so, he did not let Edward completely off the hook because he insisted that the English king build a magnificent church dedicated to St. Peter. This was undoubtedly a canny move on the part of the Pope, because the king was unlikely to leave a realm he had just retaken regardless of his oaths, and a pilgrimage was of little benefit to Rome anyway. However, the proposed church would be

---

3 Harold, often considered the last Saxon king, who lost to William at the Battle of Hastings (1066) had not completely consolidated his reign by the time he died.

richly endowed and a jewel of the Roman Catholic Church, and if its loyalty to the Vatican was ever in doubt, its dedication to St. Peter (of whom the Pope was seen as the direct spiritual descendant) confirmed its place in the Roman camp. This loyalty was of importance to the Vatican at the time because of the recent 1054 schism with the Patriarch of Constantinople, a division that would eventually lead to the foundation of the Roman Catholic and Eastern Orthodox churches.

    The King apparently agreed to the project with enthusiasm, likely because it fit within a larger plan of his own to create a grand royal compound as part of a new capital for himself. Kings in the Dark Ages were somewhat itinerant figures without fixed capitals due to the need to move from stronghold to stronghold as the needs of politics, war, or the king's whims dictated. To a degree, the king and his court were firefighters who had to travel and put down problems as they arose, all while trying to maintain the loyalty of often-rebellious barons. However, Edward sought to create a center of royal power from which he could rule over his kingdoms. The ancient rights of the City of London prevented him from making it his center of power and so he instead chose the nearby monastery of Westminster, conveniently outside of London but close enough to easily access its markets, moneylenders and similar services. The fact that the abbot of Westminster at the time, Edwin, was a close friend of the King's and that the church was already dedicated to St. Peter only sealed the deal.

    At Westminster, the king sought to create not only a magnificent church but also a new palace, both in a matching Romanesque style. The Palace of Westminster became the seat of government housing the royal court, as well as the House of Lords and the House of Commons. From that point on, Westminster Abbey has been fundamentally tied to the Crown and the English (and then British) government. This, perhaps more than any other act, defined Westminster as the royal church of England, set apart from the more purely religious seats of Canterbury and York.

    Work began on the structure, the first Romanesque church on the island of Britain, in 1055 and was pretty much complete in 1065, so Edward was able to attend its consecration a few days before his death. Edward would eventually be buried within the church that he had sponsored, the first of many tombs within the grounds, but the church was then caught up in the drama immediately succeeding Edward's death. There was a struggle for power which eventually led to an invasion by French-speaking Normans from the continent, a conflict that culminated in the Battle of Hastings (1066). At the battle, the Saxon heir to Edward's throne, King Harold, was killed during his army's defeat at the hands of William the Conqueror's invaders.

    For his coronation, William traveled to Westminster and held the ceremony, thus beginning a tradition that every English and British monarch has followed since. However, while today this ritual is done to honor the traditions of the monarchy and its connection to St. Edward the Confessor, it was probably not out of profound respect that William chose the location. Like Edward, he could have chosen any convenient cathedral for the ritual, but he seems to have chosen Westminster as a manifestation of his triumph. After all, there was no greater symbol of the victory of the Normans over the Saxons than to crown their new king in the brand-new symbol of royal Saxon power. At the same time, the fact that William claimed to be Edward's true heir (which is how he legitimized the Conquest) meant he could also say that a coronation in his predecessor's church was a rightful inheritance. One must also remember that despite the newness of the church building, the foundation of the monastery dated back four centuries at this point and was thus a place imbued with antiquity and connection to the earliest days of Saxon Christianity.

An English coin depicting William the Conqueror

This is the Bayeux Tapestry's depiction of the Church at the time of Edward's death.

Chapter 3: Henry III and the Current Construction

Medieval illustration depicting Richard II's marriage to Anne of Bohemia in 1382

For the next two centuries after the Norman Conquest, Westminster served admirably as the preeminent royal church for the realm, but there were some changes as construction on an expanded nave began in 1110 and lasted until 1163. As the 13th century dawned, another expansion was planned, and the small eastern semi-circular chapel behind the high altar was demolished and replaced with a larger lady chapel dedicated to the Virgin and consecrated in 1220. Both of these expansions were linked to the growing status of Edward the Confessor; like many Christian kingdoms, there was a tradition in Christian Saxon Britain of popular cults to deceased members of the royal family (who were treated as saints). While these cults were widespread in their day, none of these saints was officially recognized by the Catholic Church, and eventually the piety of the followers waned and they were largely forgotten. The exception to this was Edward the Confessor.

On the face of it, Edward was not a particularly likely candidate for canonization. He was famed for his violent temper, not to mention his love of war and the blood sport of hunting, all of which was frowned upon for saints. Moreover, while he had founded or built ecclesiastical structures like Westminster, this was standard behavior for Christian kings. However, it appears that popular veneration for St. Edward began almost immediately after his death, and since Westminster was the site of his relics, it quickly became a site of pilgrimage.

Understandably, official response to this cult was mixed. On the one hand, the early Norman kings were understandably leery of the veneration of a Saxon king because it could provide a potential rallying point for rebellion. On the other hand, the relics and interpretation of the cult was firmly within royal control rather than located in a distant province, and William the Conqueror had claimed descent from St. Edward as well. Thanks to that claim, the English monarchy stood to benefit from having a saintly connection.

Furthermore, English leaders understood that saints were big business in the Middle Ages, and the income from pilgrims was a major source of income for the monks of Westminster. This extra source of income was independent of royal patronage, which therefore gave them a freer hand and undoubtedly made them warmer to the possibility of Edward's canonization. Along with that, their position so close to the seat of royal power gave them added influence.

In the end, the Norman monarchs came to embrace St. Edward the Confessor, and the expansion of the nave of Westminster was the first expression of this. Edward's body was moved from whatever tomb it was kept in and placed alongside the High Altar where he was venerated, eventually pushing St. Peter, the official patron, out of the limelight. The reconstruction of the lady chapel likewise gave more space for pilgrims and worship behind the Altar, in an area with excellent views of the Saint's tomb.

As time went on, these initial expansions were viewed as insufficient, so a grand plan for reconstruction was hatched in the 13th century. Starting in 1245, under the abbots Richard Crokesley and Richard Ware and the patronage of King Henry III, the entire eastern portion of the church, including half of the nave, was demolished and completely rebuilt. For 30 years, construction continued apace until a series of disasters: the death of Henry in 1272; a terrible fire in 1298 which necessitated the reconstruction of the entire monastic complex; and the 1349 arrival of the Black Death, which devastated England as a whole and the monastic community specifically. These successive disasters led to a cessation of building for close to a century, so the nave was not completed until 1517, thanks to a boost of support under a new patron: Henry VII. This new King Henry also funded a reconstruction of the Lady Chapel which is today called the "Henry VII Lady Chapel." Henry was buried in this chapel after his death in 1509.

The effigy of Henry III in Westminster Abbey

The tomb of Henry III in Westminster Abbey

Portrait of Henry VII

Henry VII's burial was part of a general enthusiasm for monarchs to be buried within the Abbey's walls, and visitors to Westminster today are often surprised at how many people are buried within what is ostensibly a church, not an indoor cemetery or even an official national pantheon[4]. It is not even officially a royal tomb in the way many dynasties have a custom-built tomb for their royals, including el Escorial in Spain, Mauna 'Ala (the Royal Mausoleum of Hawai'i) and the Habsburg Imperial Crypt in Vienna. Westminster is not like any of these places, but it is a church where successive generations of monarchs and other prominent figures

---

4   Many nations, such as France, have a "pantheon," a temple-like structure which is built to house the remains of the nation's most illustrious figures.

have decided to be buried.

Much of the reason for this is the presence of St. Edward's relics. In the traditions of the Catholic Church, the bodies of saints are considered to contain some residue of the holiness that the man or woman possessed in life. As such, proximity to these relics conveyed some of that holy power to the everyday person. This was the reason for pilgrimage but also for the burial of the dead close to the bodies of the saint. The closer the proximity of the person to the saint, the stronger this influence was believed to be[5].

The new Church was also of a new style. The old Romanesque style was notable for its thick, short columns, its dark and small interiors, and its imperfect mimicry of old Roman styles (hence the description Romanesque). However, the new style was named for the people who first developed it: the Goths of today's France. The Gothic architecture was pioneered in French cathedrals in places like Chartres, but it also quickly became an international style that was enthusiastically adopted across the Western Christian world.

The Gothic style used pointed arches instead of the old rounded ones, as well as a technique called the "flying buttress," a support on the outer surface of the building onto which some of the stresses of holding up the outer walls can be distributed. This reconfiguring of the building's structure allowed for supports to become slimmer, further apart and fewer, which opened up unprecedented amounts of wall space for windows. This led in turn to a fluorescence of the art of stained glass. Great open walls of stained glass characterize Gothic churches, making them into glorious temples of light, all of which would have awed people of the time even more than they do for modern visitors[6].

---

5   *The Cult of the Saints: Its Rise and Function in Latin Christianity* by Peter Brown (1982)
6   "Gothic Architecture" in *The Encyclopedia Britannica.* Accessed online at: http://www.britannica.com/EBchecked/topic/239678/Gothic-architecture

Artificial light is used to draw attention to the flying buttresses.

The Gothic influences on the North façade can be seen in this picture by Zachi Evenor.

Westminster was also a site of great temporal power since the Abbot of Westminster sat on the House of Lords, giving him influence over the affairs of the realm on par with the most important lords. Locally, the Abbot was considered a feudal lord who controlled the surrounding villages and countryside, which gave him both political and economic influence. As mentioned above, the steady flow of pilgrims and royal patronage also bolstered the Abbey's coffers and influence. All of this considerable influence elicited envy, distrust and bitterness that would eventually legitimize the next era in the Abbey's history: the dissolution of the monasteries.

Chapter 4: Tudor Dissolution and an Abbey in Name Only

Portrait of Henry VIII

The dissolution of the Monasteries was one part of the much larger English Reformation. It is perhaps easy to over-simplify the Reformation by claiming that it was motivated by the English King Henry VIII's desire to divorce his various wives and remarry, but rarely does any king have the power to effect such overwhelming social change without at least some backing from the society at large. Even if Henry VIII had been able to break with the Catholic Church based solely upon his own desires, it was an innovation that would never have been able to live beyond his death.

Instead, while the desire to divorce may have been Henry's stated goal, it was a pretext. The dynasty to which Henry belonged - the Tudors - had been the victors of a vicious civil war called the War of the Roses, which was fought from 1455-1487. The kings that emerged out of that conflict were dedicated to creating a centralized state in which the monarch had tremendous power and which would hopefully avoid such conflicts in the future. As a result, the Tudor centralization affected all parts of civil governance and also extended into the realm of religion. What the Tudors did by breaking with the Catholic Church in Rome was to eliminate their greatest rival to power: the autonomous church. The wealthy priestly hierarchy would no longer be answerable to the Pope but instead to the monarch. Moreover, if the equally autonomous monastic establishments could be eliminated at the same time, then the monarch could redistribute their wealth by taking the best gems for himself (as he would with Westminster) and giving away the rest to loyal noble families, further bolstering his rule. Henry VIII correctly bargained that these families - flush with new power - would be willing to support the monarchy against any potential return of the Catholic Church (which would presumably seek to re-establish the monasteries).

At the same time that these political and economic considerations influenced Henry, there was also a new theological trend that would justify his changes: Protestantism. Henry does not appear to have been deeply influenced by Protestant theology himself (he had previously been the "Defender of the Faith" for the Pope), but he certainly used the strength of its followers. The Protestant Reformation had spread across Europe in response to the corruption, wealth and inordinate influence of the Catholic Church, and while their hatred might have been strongest towards the Pope, nowhere in Britain itself was their ire raised as it was toward the monks of the great monastic establishments like Westminster, St. Paul's and Glastonbury. Protestants looked at the centuries of treasures these places had accumulated as a cancer upon the true Christian faith.

Another impact of the Protestant Reformation was the de-emphasis placed upon the role of saints in worship. The new Anglican Church developed a complex and at times contradictory relationship with the concept of saints; while they recognized that saints did exist and were humans worthy of respect and imitation, they did not believe saints were worthy of veneration and prayer. Thus, saintly statues were removed from throughout Westminster (especially the exterior facade), as were many traditional decorations due to the fact the Protestants favored an austere decor that did not distract from the ceremony. In the vast majority of churches, saintly relics were either hidden or (more commonly) removed and destroyed, but in Westminster, St. Edward the Confessor's body remained in its place near the altar, providing yet one more reason why Westminster is distinct. This may have been due to royal protection or the fact that Edward the Confessor was considered a monarch within the traditional mausoleum of the royal family. One unintended impact of the removal of the saintly statues is that it freed up considerable space on walls and inside chapels, thereby providing more room for tombs and the commemorations of the deceased. This has certainly helped give Westminster its modern feel as a gigantic mausoleum.

Hence, when Henry VIII broke with Rome and dissolved the monasteries, he found a strong following among his allies in the nobility and among the growing number of dissidents in the Protestant faction. While monastic lands and wealth elsewhere were given to noble houses or to cathedrals under the control of loyal bishops, in Westminster, the king decided to exert his power personally. The abbots of Westminster had long been a powerful force at both the regional and national level, but the king moved to consolidate that power for himself. Thus, in 1539, Westminster Abbey was technically dissolved, and in its place, Henry created an institution called a Royal Peculiar. Westminster Abbey was not a cathedral (and it is not today), and there was no Bishop appointed to rival the great bishops of London, Canterbury or York; instead, the organization created in the time of Henry VIII - more or less still in place today - was a "Collegiate Church." The governing body is a group of clergy called a "College," the members are called " Prebendaries" ("Prebend" in singular), and they are led by an individual called the "Dean." The modern educational terms "college" and "dean" come from these institutions, which were at the heart of the original Oxford and Cambridge Universities. These priests are typically chosen from the most respected parish priests and Church administrators from the surrounding region and may or may actually preside over services at Westminster, though day-to-day religious services are generally conducted by younger, lower-ranking priests. Together, the Deacons are called the "Chapter" (akin to a Board of Directors), and they meet in the heart of the old Abbey: the Chapterhouse. In addition to Westminster, this Collegiate Church system is found in most Church of England cathedrals in Britain.

Westminster Abbey has been controlled since 1539 by the Church of England (the "C of E" to most Britons). Also called the "Anglican" or "Episcopal" Church, the Church of England has retained a unique position in Christianity because it bridges the Protestant and Catholic worlds. Anglicans are Protestant because they reject the control of the Pope, but they are Catholic because they view their priests as having a direct spiritual lineage from the Twelve Apostles and they practice the Mass. Throughout the history of England since 1539, there have been tensions between these two poles of Christian worship, and those tensions have led to bloodshed on numerous occasions.

Westminster Abbey today is very much a product of this complex history, and the impacts of it can be seen woven into the ritual, administration, art and modern uses of the building. At least in theory, the Collegiate Church preserves some of the democratic governance of the old monastic system, but in Westminster, this autonomy is greatly constrained by its position as a Royal Peculiar, which means appointment to the priestly positions from Dean on down is not done through the normal channels of the Church hierarchy but instead by the direct hand of the monarch. In essence, the Royal Peculiar of Westminster Abbey is treated in law as a private chapel serving the needs of the monarch, much in the way that local nobility throughout England traditionally had the prerogative to appoint the chaplains of their private chapels.

While Westminster "belongs" to the monarchy, the running of the institution is handled by the Dean, who inherited many of the powers of the old Abbot. Between 1585 and 1900, the Abbey (through the Dean's administration) controlled lands of the local City of Westminster and the surrounding countryside known as the Liberty of Westminster. In 1900, these powers were at least officially secularized by being transferred to a new institution called the Westminster Court of Burgesses, which was led by the High Steward of Westminster (today a ceremonial position appointed for life by the Dean and Chapter[7]).

The Abbey was a Cathedral with a bishop for a short period of time under Henry VIII. From 1540-1550, there was a Bishop of Westminster, followed by a period until 1556 when it was the co-seat along with St. Paul's of the Bishop of London. However, this was the general solution that Henry had given to all of the great Abbey Churches until he found more permanent uses for them. Likewise, there was a short-lived period under his daughter Elizabeth I when the monks were re-established and the Abbot of Westminster was the last monastic to sit on the House of Lords. However, after this period of uncertainty, the pattern of governance and worship was established at Westminster that remained continuous until the modern age.

---

[7] http://www.westminster-abbey.org/press/news/news/2011/february/lord-luce-appointed-high-steward-of-westminster-abbey

Effigy of Elizabeth I in Westminster Abbey

Chapter 5: Foundations of the Modern Church

"I should like to have seen a gallery of coronation beauties, at Westminster Abbey, confronted for a moment by this band of Island girls; their stiffness, formality, and affectation contrasted with the artless vivacity and unconcealed natural graces of these savage maidens. It would be the Venus de' Medici placed beside a milliner's doll." – Herman Melville

The final addition to the modern Abbey was the construction of the two large towers over the Great West Door in 1722. Since that time, the Abbey has mostly kept the same appearance. However, this similarity of appearance belies the major changes in use that the Abbey went through during this period.

Gordon Joly's picture of the Great West Door

One element of change was that during this period, the lands controlled by Westminster were completely absorbed into the urban conurbation of Greater London, although official control of civic affairs by the Dean and Chapter would not be removed until 1900. This absorption was one element of the Abbey's shift from being essentially an organ of government with ceremonies largely meeting the private needs of the rulers into a site for direct engagement between the government and the governed.

In addition, another development was the increasing use of burial at the Abbey as a reward for service to the nation by commoners, which occurred around the same time that the practice of royal burial ceased in 1760. Royals were joined by scientists like Sir Isaac Newton (1727),

Charles Lyell (1875), Charles Darwin (1882), and David Livingstone (1873), as well as men of letters like Robert Browning (1889), Charles Dickens (1870), Alfred Lord Tennyson (1892) and Dr. Samuel Johnson (1784). The death and interment of each of these individuals (and many others) became a national ceremony that symbolically tied the life of the individual to the nation, the state and the monarchy.

The tomb of Sir Isaac Newton

In 1725, King George I created a new honorific knightly society, the Order of the Bath. Named for a medieval tradition of giving knights a ritual purification bath akin to an adult baptism, the Order of the Bath was essentially a new organization. Its purpose was to recognize great accomplishments amongst members of the military and, to a lesser extent, the public administration. Since a reorganization of the Order in 1825, the official chapel of the Order has been the Henry VII Lady Chapel, and today the Order's banners decorate the chapel alongside seats for the 34 senior-most members of the organization[8].

Westminster Abbey with a procession of Knights of the Bath, by Canaletto (1749)

The reorganization transformed the order from a pseudo-medieval military society (with a small number of knights expected to undergo prayer vigils and coordinate the defense of the realm) to a much larger honorary society meant to reward the service of Britain's military men. The movement to the large Henry VII Chapel was part of a general conversion of Westminster Abbey during the 18th and 19th centuries into a ceremonial centerpiece for the public rituals of the monarchy, essentially a set for propaganda pageantry.

---

8   "Order of the Bath" at *The Official Website of the British Monarchy*. Accessed online at: http://www.royal.gov.uk/MonarchUK/Honours/OrderoftheBath.aspx

Nowhere was this more evident than in the evolution of the coronation ceremony. During this period, especially in the 19th century, the British government developed the essence of the modern coronation at Westminster. While there are definitely continuities between the modern ceremony and its medieval predecessors, there has actually been a major sea-change in ritual from the Victorian Period onwards. Before the 19th century, Britain was one of many monarchies in Europe vying for prestige, and one way that the British set themselves apart from the Catholic monarchies of France and Spain was by having restrained, simple ceremonies for events like coronations and royal weddings. During the Protestant Reformation (1539) and the French Revolution (1789), the British prided themselves on the rationality and simplicity of these rites, which were essentially family affairs for the Royal Family and the high nobility. However, after the French Revolution, Britain was no longer on the forefront of rationality and modernity but merely a stalwart of the old royal order. The bolstering of the legitimacy of the monarchy to the masses became a primary concern (some might even say an obsession) for the government after the Revolution in Paris and the death of Louis XVIII, so one tool they used for doing this was a massive uptick in the complexity, cost and importance of royal ceremonials. Innovations like open carriage rides through the streets for the new monarch or the newlywed royals, increased numbers of spectators, participation of the press, and now radio and television commentary of the proceedings were all essentially propaganda tools used to bolster the legitimacy of the institution of the monarchy[9]. Westminster, with its antiquity, beauty, and grand size, has served as the central stage for all of this pageantry, giving another new political role to the ancient building.

---

9   *The Invention of Tradition* by Eric Hobsbawm and Terence Ranger (1992)

Chapter 6: The Abbey in the 20th and 21st Centuries

Statues for the 20th century Christian martyrs commemorated at the Abbey

The fundamental roles of the modern Abbey were well established by the dawn of the 20th century, so it's only natural that the last 115 years have not been years of great innovation or change for the institution. This is fitting in a sense because the Abbey has come to represent continuity and tradition, and many Britons take comfort in the stalwart nature of institutions like it.

Meanwhile, the official hierarchy and institutions of the Tudor Royal Peculiar have lost much of their direct administrative power. For instance, the High Steward of Westminster no longer manages the civic government of the Borough of Westminster but is instead merely a ceremonial position and a prominent steppingstone for those moving up in the still-overlapping hierarchies of Church and State.[10]

Fortunately, Westminster does not bear the scars of the World Wars that some areas of London

---

10 https://www.churchofengland.org/media-centre/news/2012/04/archbishopric-of-canterbury-chair-of-crown-nominations-commission-appointed.aspx

and greater England suffered, due mostly to the fact that the Abbey (and its delicate stained glass) is located alongside the center of the British government, placing it within the most fiercely protected area of airspace in the entire country. During the Battle of Britain, the treasures of the church were sent to safe locations in the north, while the toms were covered in sandbags for their protection. While St. Paul's to the east was at times wreathed in smoke and flame, Westminster was spared most of this destruction, though the Abbey was home to a group of volunteers who slept in the Nave every night with firefighting equipment in order to put out any incendiary bombs that happened to make their way into the structure. One set of incendiary bombs did penetrate during German attacks, but the damage was minimal. The Abbey was also the site of the official state prayer on VE Day (the day Germany surrendered), with roughly 25,000 attendees[11].

Westminster is still legally a Royal Peculiar and serves foremost the needs of the Royal Family. The first time the world at large really got a good look at Westminster was for the coronation of Elizabeth II in 1953, the first British royal coronation ceremony to be filmed for television and a major cultural milestone not only in Britain but throughout the world. The soaring backdrop of Westminster, redolent in antiquity and bursting with the elite of the dying British Empire, made an impression on all who watched the proceedings.

While there have been no royal burials in Westminster since George in 1760 - today the royal family entombs its dead in the roomier confines of Windsor Castle - it has continued to serve for the far more joyous occasions of royal weddings. Weddings occurred here infrequently during the Middle Ages, especially in the 1200s, but between 1382 and 1919, there were no royal weddings in Westminster. In 1919, however, Westminster again became the principal site for royal unions, perhaps the most important new development in the 20th century history of the Abbey. There have been 10 such wedding since then,[12] and the most important of these were the ceremonies for heirs, including the marriage of Princess (now Queen) Elizabeth to Philip, Duke of Edinburgh in 1947, and the marriage of Prince William to Kate Middleton in 2011[13]. In both of these events, Westminster served as the stage for royal pageantry, dramatic photos, and general national pride Britain.

The Abbey Church has also been the site of numerous funerals, including all of the hundreds of individuals interred at the site. In recent years, there have also been state funerals for individuals who were not interred there, including Queen Elizabeth (the "Queen Mother"), Diana, Princess of Wales, and Queen Alexandra (wife of King Edward VII). The funeral of Princess Diana in particular was an event of international scope equal to that of the most important weddings and coronations.

---

11 "History: War Damage" http://www.westminster-abbey.org/our-history/war-damage
12 As well as four more in the medieval period.
13 The wedding of Prince Charles to Lady Diana Spencer in 1981 was held in St. Paul's Cathedral.

Chapter 7: Tour of the Church

"As I passed along the side walls of Westminster Abbey, I hardly saw any thing but marble monuments of great admirals, but which were all too much loaded with finery and ornaments, to make on me at least, the intended impression." – Karl Philipp Moritz

Although it is not London's largest church, an honor goes to the mighty St. Paul's in the old City of London, the Abbey is an undoubtedly impressive structure. The giant Abbey is 531 feet (162 meters) long, and at its widest point (the transept) it is 203 feet (62 meters) wide. The space under the nave and transept is roughly 80 feet (24 meters) across. The main building stands 102 feet (31 meters) high, and the tops of the two towers above the great gate are 225 feet (69 meters) tall. Overall, when viewed from above, the building takes the form of a Latin Cross (a simple cross with a longer lower part and a single crosspiece)[14]. This type of form is not uncommon amongst the great churches of the Latin Christian tradition[15] and is the church shape that is generally pictured when people imagine a cathedral.

---

14 "Westminster Abbey" at *How Stuff Works* accessed online at:
http://geography.howstuffworks.com/europe/westminster-abbey.htm
15 Which includes both Roman Catholicism - the Church that built Westminster - and also Anglicanism, the Church that has worshipped in the structure for the majority of its history

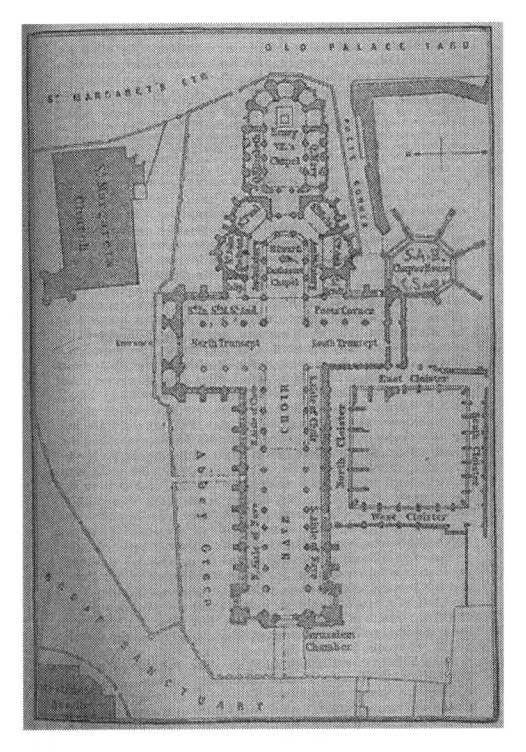

This 19th century layout indicates the Latin Cross shape of the Abbey.

Visitors to the church generally approach the structure from the west, in the large open courtyard that surrounds the structure. They are advised that the Abbey is not a museum or a monument but first and foremost a working Church, so during the multiple daily ceremonies, they are asked to respect the sacred proceedings and not make unnecessary noise. That said, visitors are also invited to participate in the ceremonies, and many who are not even Christian do so in order to enjoy the music (pipe organs and boys choirs) and ceremonials of the ancient rituals of Mass and Evensong which have occurred here daily for over a millennium. Indeed, it is one of the most ancient halls of Christian worship in the British Isles[16].

Great West Door

Flanked by two mighty towers, the Great West Door is a truly impressive entryway. The front facade of the structure is worth looking at in itself. One knows that this building is a product of the Protestant Reformation due to the fact that all along the exterior are niches that once held

---

16 *Westminster Abbey Homepage.* Accessed online at: http://www.westminster-abbey.org/

statues of saints which were removed by the more zealous Reformers. While the statues are gone, the niches remain as a reminder of this "iconoclastic[17]" period of Church history. Today it is here that visitors purchase tickets and buy souvenirs before entering.

The Great West Door

The Nave

Upon entering the Abbey, visitors encounter the Nave, the long main body of the church which was completely rebuilt in the 13th century with the then-cutting edge Gothic style. As a result, the walls are high and made up of a forest of arches with pointed tops and seemingly countless stained glass windows. Stained glass was a distinctive characteristic of the Gothic style, and the windows in the Abbey bathe the interior spaces of places like the Nave with beautiful colored light and illuminating Bible stories, lives of saints, and similar pious images for the illiterate faithful.[18]

---

17 This term means "icon-breaking" and in its original form meant a religious movement that destroyed the images of saints or gods as they saw them as heretical. Many strongly Protestant faiths are fiercely iconoclastic, as is the Sunni Muslim tradition, especially in the modern Wahhabi sect.
18 "Westminster Abbey" at *The New Catholic Encyclopedia*. Accessed online at: http://www.newadvent.org/cathen/15598a.htm

Many would agree that the best time to enter the Nave is during one of the regular performances of the pipe organs. Installed for the coronation of King George VI in 1937, it is only the latest of a series of ever-grander organs dating back to at least 1304. Like all of the great Gothic churches, Westminster was designed with an organ in mind, and the building is essentially part of the instrument. The stones of the grand hall resound with the organ's music, which appears to come from nowhere and everywhere as the walls themselves vibrate. The music penetrates and, if performed the way it is intended, enhances the spiritual power of the structure. The list of official Organists of Westminster Abbey, an old position in the hierarchy, has included some of the finest musicians in English history, including the masterful John Blow and Henry Purcell. Even today, the Summer Organ Festival brings the modern masters together in the old Abbey Church[19].

Although the Nave is one of the outermost areas of the Abbey, visitors can't help but notice the large number of tombs and memorials covering the walls and floors. The Royals are clustered closer to the High Altar, but in the Nave, the most famous of these tombs is that of Sir Isaac Newton. This tomb includes a statue of the great physicist with the implements of his trade: books, a globe, and an apple[20].

Quire

The Quire ("Choir" in American English) is a place where the great antiquity of Westminster first begins to confront most visitors. The Nave is awe-inspiring, but the wooden quire stalls, used by centuries of choirboys, priests, and dignitaries, are full of history.[21] The quire is akin to a wooden building without a ceiling that is set in the center of the nave, and the structure has two entry archways: one facing the High Altar and the other facing the Great West Door. This means that during formal ceremonies (everything from Easter to a Royal Wedding), groups of priests and worshippers can proceed along the nave all the way to the Altar. On both sides of the central processual aisle are several rows of beautiful, hand carved wooden seats. The highest seats have tall backs that meld into the woodwork of the walls, all of which are topped by the medieval banners of the Order of Bath. During ceremonies, the lower seats of the choir - those closest to the aisle - are filled with red and white robed choirboys. In everyday events like the nightly Evensong, the rest of the choir seats are filled with worshipers, but during rituals of national importance, they fill up with bishops and other church dignitaries.

Cloisters and the Cloister Garden

---

19 "Music and the Choir: The Organ" at the homepage of *Westminster Abbey* accessed online at: http://www.westminster-abbey.org/music/organ
20 "History: Sir Isaac Newton" at the homepage of *Westminster Abbey* accessed online at: http://www.westminster-abbey.org/our-history/people/david-livingstone
21 "Westminster Abbey" at *The Encyclopedia Britannica*. Accessed online at: http://www.britannica.com/EBchecked/topic/641068/Westminster-Abbey

Bernard Gagnon's picture of the cloister

Those seeking a full tour of the Abbey should duck out of the main sanctuary at this time and exit the building through one of several doors on the southern side. These lead to the rooms of the old monastic compound, today used primarily for administrative purposes. It has both above-ground and subterranean rooms available for visitors to view.

While the monks and Abbots are long gone - victims of the Protestant Reformation in 1539 - there are many reminders of their life in this area of the complex, especially the cloister garden. The "cloister" was the area of the monastery that was off-limits to all but the monks and their invited guests, and at the center of it is a square courtyard with a center of grass and plants that is surrounded by a raised stone walkway with a roof supported by columns (a "colonnade"). The monks would circumnavigate the courtyard in a form of mobile prayer and contemplation that many found useful for communion with God. In the Middle Ages, this was a place of escape and respite from the hustle and bustle of the Abbey church, and it remains an oasis even today.[22]

Abbey Museum and the Pyx Chamber

---

22 "Westminster Abbey (The Collegiate Church of St Peter)" in the *National Heritage List for England.* On the homepage of English Heritage. Accessed online at: http://list.english-heritage.org.uk/resultsingle.aspx?uid=1291494

Beyond the cloister garden and further into the old monastic structures are two rooms that might attract the interest of tourists: the Abbey Museum and the Pyx Chamber. Both of these are located in historic monastic rooms, but there is little evidence of the monks here.

The Abbey Museum is remarkable because it holds the treasures of Westminster. The modern museum is located in the "undercroft," a subterranean area that was a storage facility in the medieval monastery, and it includes objects like effigies made of the royal dead, other funerary items, stained glass, a rare original statue of St. Peter, and altarpieces. The lack of gold and silver objects is largely due to the fact that many such medieval objects were considered to be too "popish" (Catholic) in the Reformation and were thus destroyed. Furthermore, despite the Abbey's connection with coronations, the Crown Jewels are not held in this location but are instead kept under protected lock and key in the Tower of London in the old City of London downriver[23].

Picture of an empty effigy in the Abbey

Next to the Abbey Museum is the Pyx Chamber. The Pyx is a container (often in the form of a

---

[23] "Visiting the Abbey: The Museum" at the *Westminster Abbey Homepage.* Accessed online at: http://www.westminster-abbey.org/visit-us/highlights/the-museum

call made of precious metals) which was traditionally suspended on chains above the High Altar along with a lit candle in its interior. This device was used in the Middle Ages and continues to be used in Catholic churches and in some highly traditionalist Anglican settings. It is used to hold the Host (blessed Communion wafers) between Mass, and the priest could draw upon this supply of wafers when traveling to visit the homes of the sick and invalid who could not physically attend Church but were still able to enjoy the benefits of Holy Communion.

The pyxes on display at the Abbey served another use. They were similar boxes, but they were created to house coins which were stored for an annual trial during which royal officials tested the coins for their purity of gold and silver. However, the minting and testing of the coins was done not by Church officials; instead, the Exchequer produced the coins and a city guild called the Worshipful Company of Goldsmiths tested them. It is an example of the deep intersection between church and state in the United Kingdom[24].

While the Pyx Chamber is often overlooked by modern visitors to the Church, the pyx as a religious implement (rather than one of measuring coinage) has long been a spot for rancorous debate in the Anglican Church. Today, and for many centuries now, the Church is divided between those who view Mass as a symbolic ritual meant to assist prayer (the "Low" Church, those with more Protestant tendencies) and those who see the Mass as a miraculous event where the Host becomes literally imbued with the essence of Christ (the "High" Church, those with more Catholic tendencies). This debate, while it seems rather silly to many even within the Church today, was one of the theological sources of the Great Schism within the Anglican Church that led to the English Civil Wars. Westminster Abbey has always had a greater High Church tendency since it is associated with medieval pageantry and the rituals of the monarchy, and this bias is revealed by the presence of the pyxes within the modern church, a feature that is lacking from many ordinary Anglican parishes.

Chapter House

---

24 "Visiting the Abbey: The Pyx Chamber" at the *Westminster Abbey Homepage*. Accessed online at: http://www.westminster-abbey.org/visit-us/highlights/the-pyx-chamber

The Chapter House

If the High Altar is the spiritual heart of Westminster, the Chapter House is its political focal point, and Westminster has always been at the center of English and British political life. The Chapter House is located in the old monk's cloister complex and is a room set off from the main area of the cloister by a hallway. This round open chamber was once the meeting room for the monks of Westminster, the place where the Abbot addressed his fellows, the spot where new abbots were chosen, and the site where the most important spiritual and political decisions were made. After the suppression of the monks, the building was renamed for the "Chapter," the assembly of the Dean of Westminster and the prebendaries for their regular meetings, along with other important groups like the King's Great Council and the early House of Commons. The room could be compared to a board room of a major corporation or charity, and it's fair to say the modern Chapter controls a large endowment and a number of employees and institutions. In fact, the Chapter now meets in a modern board room, and this room is open to the general public[25].

Poets' Corner

Picture of Poets' Corner

After leaving the relatively small spaces of the cloister, even the Chapter House seems small in comparison to the vastness of the sanctuary. Visitors can reenter the Abbey church from the south end of the transept and get an excellent side view ahead of the sacarum and the Shrine of St. Edward the Confessor. However, tour guides always ask visitors to head right to the southeastern corner of the transept, the location of a famous area called Poets' Corner. The administration of the Abbey has attempted over the centuries to invite England's most prestigious writers to have Westminster be the site of their burials, and while many have turned the invitation down, this is still perhaps the most impressive collection of literary figures in the English-speaking world.

The first literary burial to take place here was for Geoffrey Chaucer (1343-1400), the great

---

25 "Visiting the Abbey: The Chapter House" at the *Westminster Abbey Homepage.* Accessed online at: http://www.westminster-abbey.org/visit-us/highlights/the-chapter-house

royal poet who is considered by many to be the first great master of the English language. His masterpiece, *Canterbury Tales*, is still read to this day, even though the language has evolved so much over the centuries that it must often be read in translation into modern English. When Chaucer was interred here, the vicinity was not considered to belong to poets, but it was a desire of later generations to be buried close to the great master, akin to the way that later monarchs desired to be buried close to the venerated remains of St. Edward. The most well-known of those in Poets' corner include Ben Jonson (1572-1637), the playwright and contemporary of Shakespeare who was buried upright, the 17th century Poet Laureate John Dryden, and 19th century poet Robert Browning. Today, the tradition continues of memorializing (though not burying as space no longer permits) major writers and artists, such as C.S. Lewis and the founders of the Royal Ballet.

Sacarum and the Shrine of St. Edward the Confessor

The name "sacarum" is derived from Latin and roughly translates to "sacred place." This is the location of the High Altar, the focal point of every one of the great rituals performed in the Abbey since its foundation some 1,400 years ago. Like the Quire, the Sacarum has the feel of being a separate room; it has high walls but no ceiling, and it is divided from the main part of the nave by both stairs and decorative metal gratings. Visitors may ascend the steps into the Sacarum, but it's important to remember that the areas directly around the High Altar (called the "chancel") are only available for priests to walk on.

The great attraction here is not the Altar itself but the tomb located alongside it: the last resting place of King Edward the Confessor. Edward's place of pride is due to his unique historical status as England's only canonized monarch, not to mention the fact he was responsible for the construction of the first major church and palace at Westminster. Edward is still recognized as a saint among both the Anglicans and Catholics since his canonization occurred before the splintering of those faiths.

Henry VII's Lady Chapel

Behind (to the east of) and around the Sacarum is the Lady Chapel, rebuilt during the reign of King Henry VII (1457–1509), the first monarch of the Tudor dynasty. The last area of the Abbey Church to be built, it was created in a late Gothic Period style called the "Perpendicular Gothic."

The Chapel was dedicated to the Virgin Mary (the "Lady") and is famous for its remarkably beautiful fan ceiling. A fan ceiling is a form of structure where the room's supporting pillars split at their crowns like trees with multiple branches. These branches then fan out across the room, eventually meeting up with and merging into the branches of other altars. This gives a classic "ribbed" look to the ceiling. The Lady Chapel of Westminster is one of the finest examples of the style.

Within the Lady Chapel and the surrounding side chapels are buried an impressive number of monarchs. Desiring to be buried close to St. Edward, their holy ancestor, they cluster here behind the High Altar, primarily in raised stone tombs. The names here are often well-known: William III, Charles II, Henry VII, and the infamous half-sisters Mary, Queen of Scots and Elizabeth I, whose bloody rivalry - much of it relating to religious differences over Protestantism and Catholicism - almost led the kingdom into civil war in the 16th century. The viciousness of their mutual opposition is belied by the locations of their tombs, as the two queens lie close to each other in the Lady Chapel. Almost every English monarch was buried here until George II, who died in 1760. After George II, all subsequent monarchs were buried in Windsor Castle, if only because there simply wasn't enough room at Westminster.

One notable side chapel is the Royal Air Force (RAF) Chapel, which includes stained glass depictions of the Battle of Britain in 1940. Naturally, it commemorates the RAF's defense of the homeland against the German Luftwaffe and prevented a potential ground invasion of the British Isles.[26]

Perhaps the most infamous burial in the Lady Chapel was Oliver Cromwell, who headed the revolutionary government of the Commonwealth as the Lord Protector from 1653-1658. The only non-royal head of state in British history, he was given a full state burial after his death in the Chapel, but when the monarchy returned to power in 1660, his body was exhumed and posthumously executed[27].

---

[26] "The Lady Chapel" at the homepage of *Westminster Abbey* accessed online at: http://www.westminster-abbey.org/visit-us/highlights/the-lady-chapel

[27] "History: Oliver Cromwell and Family" at the homepage of *Westminster Abbey* accessed online at: http://www.westminster-abbey.org/visit-us/highlights/the-lady-chapel

A portrait of Cromwell

Transept and the Great North Door

Just within the Great North Door is a memorial to the United Kingdom's fallen military servicemen and women, a stone set in the floor that is usually surrounded by poppies (a symbol of bloodshed in battle in Britain and the British Commonwealth). This is only one of two prominent Tombs of the Unknown Warrior in London, the other being the Cenotaph in the old City of London where the yearly commemoration of Armistice Day occurs. While that larger monument takes place of pride in major ceremonies, its location in the center of a busy street makes it less accessible than this one in Westminster, which is an understandably popular stop for visitors to the Abbey.

Visitors with enough time can also find a number of other prominent non-Royal burials at Westminster. David Livingstone, the famed African explorer whose disappearance in 1865 led to a continent-spanning search by the American journalist Henry Stanley in 1871, was buried in the Abbey. Considered to be one of the greatest Britons of his day, after his death he was offered a space of honor in the Abbey near the Nave. While his heart was buried under a mpundu tree in today's Zambia, his embalmed body was carried by his attendants to the coast and was shipped to London[28].

Dr. Livingstone

St. Margaret's Church and the Surrounding Grounds

Alongside the great bulk of Westminster Abbey is a small stone building that is reminiscent of an English country church, and it is often completely overlooked by visitors. For worshipers seeking spiritual solace or students of the history of the British Parliament, however, there are few places that compare to the tranquil interior of St. Margaret's Church.

St. Margaret's was built in the same late Gothic style as Henry VII's Lady Chapel in the Abbey and was given over in 1614 to be the parish church of the Parliament's lower house, the House of Commons. The relatively lowly construction of the church of St. Margaret's in comparison to its

---

[28] "History: David Livingstone" at the homepage of *Westminster Abbey* accessed online at:
http://www.westminster-abbey.org/our-history/people/david-livingstone

neighbor is evidence of the formerly overwhelming power of the monarchy in British politics. The fact that the House of Commons is now the dominant institution of government is put into stark context when St. Margaret's indicates how far that body has risen over the last four centuries[29].

St. Margaret's

---

29 "St. Margaret's Church" at the homepage of *Westminster Abbey* accessed online at: http://www.westminster-abbey.org/st-margarets

Another important structure located on the grounds of the Abbey is the Westminster School, a world-renowned private Church of England (Anglican) school dedicated to educating the British elite. The construction of private schools like this is common throughout the Anglican Communion, and similar institutions can be found attached to cathedrals and even parish churches throughout Britain[30].

Another school associated with the Abbey is the Choir School, which trains and educates the boys to sing in the choir for the Abbey. An ancient Anglican tradition, that choir attends all religious services at the Abbey - from coronations to nightly Evensong - providing a beautiful and uniquely Anglican sound to the ancient halls[31].

Westminster Abbey continues to serve as the personal chapel of the House of Windsor, but it can safely be said that its everyday role is to serve as one of Britain's most important tourist destinations. Visitors who are not attending a religious ceremony such as Mass or Evensong are required to purchase an entry ticket near the Great West Door, in an alcove of the entrance that also has a small gift shop. Audio guides in various languages can be rented at the same time, or visitors can join in regular guided tours. During the open hours, the Abbey swarms with visitors, but this should not be viewed too harshly since the Abbey was a structure designed for precisely that purpose. If anything, it would be strange to see the Abbey empty of worshipers and visitors.

Tourism means the Abbey is a major moneymaker for the Church of England (with over a million visitors annually), and it also theoretically serves as a form of Christian evangelism for the masses. Like the medieval pilgrims, many modern visitors come to commune with the dead, though they are more likely to be delighted by Sir Isaac Newton than St. Edward the Confessor, and they will likely be more intrigued by Elizabeth I than the pious Henry VII.

Regardless, the Abbey's status as a premiere historical and religious site has been recognized by a number of bodies. It was given the United Kingdom's highest level of historical protection, "Grade I" listing on the Statutory List of Buildings of Special Architectural or Historic Interest, in 1958. An even greater honor was bestowed in 1987 when it was added to the United Nations Educations, Cultural and Scientific Organization's (UNESCO) list of World Heritage Sites, a tally of the most important sites in world history.[32]

Bibliography

Bradley, S. and N. Pevsner (2003) The Buildings of England – London 6: Westminster, New Haven: Yale University Press, pp. 105–207.

---

30 Westminster School Homepage. Accessed online at: http://www.westminster.org.uk/
31 "Choir School" at the homepage of *Westminster Abbey* accessed online at: http://www.westminster-abbey.org/choir-school
32 "Palace of Westminster and Westminster Abbey including Saint Margaret's Church" at the *UNESCO World Heritage Site List*. Accessed online at: http://whc.unesco.org/en/list/426

Mortimer, Richard ed., Edward the Confessor: The Man and the Legend, The Boydell Press, 2009. Eric Fernie, 'Edward the Confessor's Westminster Abbey', pp. 139–150. Warwick Rodwell, 'New Glimpses of Edward the Confessor's Abbey at Westminster', pp. 151–167. Richard Gem, Craftsmen and Administrators in the Building of the Confessor's Abbey', pp. 168–172.

Harvey, B. (1993) Living and Dying in England 1100–1540: The Monastic Experience, Ford Lecture series, Oxford: Clarendon Press.

Morton, H. V. [1951] (1988) In Search of London, London: Methuen.

Trowles, T. (2008) Treasures of Westminster Abbey, London: Scala.

Made in the
USA
Columbia, SC